My Story

Cheryl Miloe

Sunesis Ministries Ltd

My Story

Published by Sunesis Ministries Ltd
Email: info@stuartpattico.com
Website: www.stuartpattico.com

ISBN: 978-0-9566864-7-3

Acknowledgements

ST Johns Wood Church.
ST Johns The Baptist Church (Essex)
The Commonwealth Church
Christian Fellowship Worship Team

I would also like to thank Jan for all her ministry.

CONTENTS

Chapter One

NEW BEGINNING

Before you start this little book I have to let you know that I am not a writer - and never had any intention of writing! When I did say to my kids that I was going to write a book one day, they just laughed - knowing how bad I am at English! Yet here I am, writing.

It's hard to start writing when you have no experience of the way in which a book should be written. But this little book is not about fancy words, accurate grammar and perfect English - it's about a wonderful journey that I want to share with whoever reads it.

We are all born in different beds to different families, whether rich or poor, educated or uneducated, good or bad. Each of us took different routes to adulthood. We all grew in different ways, had different upbringings, different experiences and walked different paths. Some of us change direction; some stay stuck in a rut and just accept things as they are.

I believe that somewhere along the path of our lives we

become lost - not all of us, but the majority.

We come to a place where we start reassessing our lives and asking questions about our happiness. Some of us look right back to problems in childhood; others just question the here and now. The trigger for this reflection on our lives could be a bereavement, a divorce or broken relationship, a move to a new place, the loss of a job or a close friendship, an affair, an illness, an accident - the list is endless. But some kind of change or crisis in our lives makes us take stock and look inwards.

Many people just plod on with no happiness or peace, perhaps because life has become a familiar routine and many fear change more than they desire change. Fear is a big factor in life - it comes in all shapes and sizes. Some people's fears are greater than others. Sometimes we don't even know where it comes from but it's there. For some it hits us like a bolt from the blue, and for others it's just a normal, everyday, expected part of life - something we put up with but have never dealt with.

For me, it came like a bolt of lightning.

In 2003, I experienced a serious panic attack. It was completely unexpected. I did not know what it was, other than it was the most frightening experience I had ever had.

It was the day I got the keys to my new home. I felt weird all day. I know some say moving is stressful, but I never get stressed over things like that. I welcome having a new home, because I love all the interior decorating aspect of it.

I picked up the keys in the afternoon and went to the supermarket to buy some cleaning stuff. Then, bang! It just came on me. I thought I was having a heart attack, and I felt I was suffocating. It was awful. Before I knew it, I was taken away in an ambulance. I was so frightened of what was happening and how I was feeling.

After many medical checks, the nurse came in and told me that I'd had a severe panic attack, and should talk to someone. From that moment I began to experience a whole load of new fears - from fear of dying and leaving my kids behind, to stepping out of the front door. I was even frightened to eat certain foods. From that day on, I constantly had terrible panic attacks. There was never a moment I was free of them.

Everything seemed to go wrong in my life from that point onwards. Maybe it had all been going wrong before, and I had just been in denial, but either way, my life was now a shambles.

My husband kept telling me it was our new home, that it was cursed because it was number 13. What had seemed to be a happy family was no longer. All of my life was falling apart, bit by bit. My panic attacks become so severe that I did not want to go out or go to work. When I did, I felt I couldn't breathe and just wanted to get home.

I looked everywhere for help, but nothing worked. I then told myself that this is my life now, this is how it is going to be. It was not a life - I was just existing, and the only reason I wanted to exist now was for my two lovely kids. They were my only concern.

We started the work needed on our home, but I could not get into it like before. Even though I managed to make the rooms look beautiful, it meant nothing to me because the feelings I was having were awful. They had taken over my life. It wasn't just the panic attacks themselves. On top of that I felt like I had a constant weight on top of me, a dread, a heaviness which is very hard to explain. If I met friends, I had to leave within minutes of meeting them. Everything in my life was affected by my condition.

The home was finished and looked stunning, but I hated living there. I hated every waking day, but I didn't have the strengh to do anything about it. I thought that so long as everyone else is happy, that's all that matters. But were they? Or did my kids look at me and think, "What's happening to our mum?"

I went from someone who was creative, talented and bubbly, to this shivering, fearful wreck. I was there physically for my kids, but it must have seemed to them like I was someone else - not the same mother they had known before.

This went on for four long years. Four years of someone's life is a very long time to suffer in that way. It's awful for anyone to suffer, but this made me question everything about myself, my life and where it was going.

One Saturday, I went to my mum's. My mother knew everything about my situation, my feelings and what was going on in my life. On this occasion she gave me the 'phone number of a friend whose name was Jan. Jan asked my mum to get me to call her the next day, Sunday, at 2pm. I was curious, and couldn't wait to see what this this lady wanted to talk to me about.

On Sunday morning I felt that all I was doing was looking at the clock I could not wait for 2pm to come around, even though I wasn't sure who this woman was or why she wanted to talk to me. At dead on two, I called Jan. She asked me if I would like to meet her. I wanted to go there and then, but it wasn't convenient for Jan, so we arranged to meet on the Monday at my mum's.

By this time I had tried everything - herbal remedies, healing therapies, reading books about my condition, breathing exercises, counselling - but nothing helped me. I was still not ready to give up, even though I couldn't see any way out of the situation I was in.

On Monday morning I didn't say anything to anyone about it. I just went to my mum's, and there she was. Jan was totally different to how I imagined her. She was beautiful, friendly and so welcoming. Mum went out, so it was just Jan and I. We spoke about other things for a bit, and then Jan asked me if I believed in God. My answer to that was, "Yes, but I'm not a religious person. I don't go to church or read the Bible, but I have always felt sensitive to certain things."

Jan explained so much to me about God and how he works. It was very interesting, but hard to believe. Then Jan asked if I wanted to give my heart to God. I was a bit confused about this, but because of what was going on in my life I would have done anything to get help. So I said yes. Jan got me to read a prayer from a yellow piece of paper. She asked me to read it aloud, which I did - and meant every word.

Jan now prayed for me, and told me I would experience deliverance from my condition, but in the process I might feel tiredness, tearfulness or depression, and it could take weeks or months. Well, everything she told me was correct, except how long it lasted. I experienced every one of those feelings, but my deliverance was immediate. When I left my mum's place, I was waiting for the usual panic attack to kick in, and it simply was not happening. The heaviness had gone!

I started to feel really different, and in a bit of shock at the realisation of what had happened. I was amazed at how I felt after Jan prayed for me.

Then, two days after seeing Jan, I had a spirtual experience that is hard to explain. I know that everyone's experience of God is different and many find it hard to describe, but when it happens it is not only very powerful at the time, but life-changing from then on. And so it was with me. I was overwhelmed.

Incredibly, I started feeling normal again. I was coming back to life, like a spring flower breaking through the hard ground, leaving behind the dark of winter and feeling the warmth of the sun.

If God had to allow those panic attacks in order to bring me to himself, then it was worth it, because the peace I was feeling was nothing like anything I had ever experienced before.

Chapter Two

ESCAPING MARITAL ABUSE

Even though I had given my heart to God and the panic attacks and feelings of fear had ended, things were still not right in my home.

I found out my husband was having yet another affair. It was ten years since his last affair, and this affair was very similar - but it was much worse than before. But if his pattern of behaviour was similar, so was mine. I repeated the way I had responded to his previous affairs, humiliations and abuse. Instead of challenging him to change, I just despaired, and allowed him to stay in the home.

But this time there was a difference - God was in my life.

Things were still really hard in our relationship. It had become a really unhappy home, and I only stayed with him for the sake of our two kids. My husband's behaviour was awful - it was mental torture. I was seeing it more and more. But each day I prayed, and every day I felt that God was making me a little bit stronger. Despite the terrible situation I was in, there was no way I was going to react against God, blaming him for it. I knew he had rescued me from the panic attacks, and I was sure he had a better future for me.

Little by little, I started dealing with all the things that needed to change. I knew it was not going to be easy. Just because I had got to know God did not mean he was going to suddenly wave some magic wand over my life and make it all perfect. I now know that's not how it works, even if I wished for that at the time. But I did believe that God was at work in my life, and so I had a confidence that I could start to change, and that he would support me and strengthen me.

I started thinking over previous situations in my marriage. I realised that the marriage had broken down long ago, and I should have walked out years earlier, but fear had held me back. Fear kept me in denial about the real situation, and I was always putting everyone else's happiness before my own. Whilst that can be a good, generous thing to do in a normal situation, in my case it became so extreme I had become a doormat - trampled over. I was beginning to see that I had to trust God to help me overcome all my fears - including this one.

Psalm 27:1 says: "The Lord is my light and my salvation - so why should I be afraid? The Lord is my fortress, protecting me from danger, so why should I tremble?"

The whole situation had become unbearable because I had allowed it to continue for so many years under my own nose, in my own home. As a result, my husband lost all respect for me. I suppose it all became easy for him because he knew I would not speak up, because I was afraid. Even though he was the bully, I became laughable - not only to my husband but also to the other woman.

I finally found the strengh to get my husband to leave. I could no longer cave in to his threats and put up with his behaviour. It was best for both of us to separate. The marriage was over. I had been dragged through the mud too many times.

My heart had been broken ten years earlier by the previous affair, not only because of the betrayal and humiliation, but because of how he treated me as a human being. The way he spoke to me was diabolical - he was always saying negative things about me. But for some strange reason, when he did say those things I used to feel sorry for him, and felt he did not mean it. I kidded myself that it was his own issues that made him act like that. After years of all that, I had become a weak, cowardly person. It was my own fault, because we are in control of our own lives and they are formed by the decisions we make. Yet we can, out of fear, come under the control of others. You become a slave to whatever or whoever controls you.

My husband finally left the home. But now I had a new problem - selling it. I did not want to spend another moment in that place. From beginning to end, living in that home had been hell.

I put the home on the market and many people viewed it, but put in silly offers for it. We were in the middle of a recession and prices were low, so they wanted to see how low I would go. I was so desperate for a new start that I was tempted to take one of those offers. I even considered taking the worst offer of all, because of how quick they wanted to move in. But I had to keep trusting God and having faith that he would bring the right person along.

Proverbs 3:5-6 says: "Trust in the Lord with all your heart; do not depend on your own understanding. Seek his will in all you do, and he will show you which path to take." I truly believed that God's timing would be perfect.

Yet it was hard to trust at that time. I was totally drained by several difficult things that came along all at the same time. There never seemed to be an end to them. Besides the marriage breakdown and the cumulative effects of 20 years of an abusive marriage, my Nan died, my kids' dog died, my poor kids and their world was turned upside down by their parents' split, and they were both in the middle of their exams! And then I had the stress of trying to move house.

Yet this is exactly what Jesus predicted. He says in John 16:33: “Here on earth you will have many trials and sorrows. But take heart, because I have overcome the world.”

I was seeing God's activity in my life, and the more I was experiencing it the more I was becoming stronger in faith. Even though things around me seemed to be falling apart, I knew God was working for good in my life. God knows everything about our situation, and works everything together for good - if we keep trusting him. He uses people and situations to save us and shape us. We are all different individuals with different circumstances and problems, so God deals with us individually. What he shows you about yourself will be different to what he shows others about themselves, because we all took different paths before we came to him.

For me, I was told that I would be stripped down so that he could put me back together in the right way. I had so much to learn about myself, and it would not be an overnight process. I would go through so much deliverance, and sometimes it might be so hard that I might want to give up my new faith.

Did that all come true? Well, here's the list:

1. I was being stripped - correct.
2. I was learning things about myself - correct. And when I did not change or listen, I found myself back in the same situations until I learned and changed.
3. It has not been an overnight process - correct. In fact it's been a real struggle and battle.
4. I went through so much deliverance - correct. And there are still times now that God takes me through more deliverance.
5. Yes it was hard, but the only thing that has not happened is that I have never wanted to give up my faith. And that makes me even more convinced that God's work in my life is real. In John 3:6-7 Jesus describes the experience of becoming a Christian as a miraculous gift from God, bringing such a radical change to our lives that it is like being born all over again. He says: "Humans can reproduce only human life, but the Holy Spirit gives birth to spiritual life. So don't be surprised when I say, 'You must be born again.'" In 2 Corinthians 6:2 God says: "At just the right time, I heard you. On the day of salvation, I

helped you." And Jesus did save me at just the right time.

I was also told that, to enable me to grow as a Christian, God would remove the people he wanted to remove from my life and put the people he wants in my life - all correct. But that doesn't mean that all the people he might put there for you are all nice people! They might just be put there to teach you something about yourself or a re-occurring issue that you need to deal with.

Anyway, back to the house move. After many months of unreasonable offers, and praying on my knees, I had a lovely couple come to my home one Saturday. Within two hours of their visit, I had a call from their agent, offering the full asking price, and we set a date to move! The buyer was called Mr Goodkind. Did the buyer live up to his name or what?! He was not only good, he was kind with it. He kept his word in every way, following through on everything he said. Praise the Lord!

On 25th January 2010 I moved out of that home.

As much as I had hated living there, I did have some lovely neighbours. One neighbour really cared for me in my time of trouble. She would bring in lovely soups she had made, and genuinely cared. It was a chink of light in a dark time.

But I wanted to get rid of everything in the house that reminded me of that period of my life. Everything went to the charity shops - even the kids bagged up everything they no longer wanted. I tried to share out all our belongings between all the local charity shops. As I was clearing out my stuff, I was clearing out my old life. It reminded me of Jesus' answer to the rich man who asked him how to get eternal life. Jesus told him to leave his past life behind, and to get rid of all that he had previously depended on so that he could depend only on God: "Go and sell all your possessions and give the money to the poor, and you will have treasure in heaven. Then come, follow me" (Matthew 19:21).

Even though my house move was a big event for me, it was far from being the end of change for me. It was just the beginning. I was still coming to the place in my life where God could teach me.

Chapter Three

MY FIRST TEACHING

After selling up, we had to move in with my mum in Essex. I felt so relieved that the home had gone, along with most of my possessions. There wouldn't have been space for them in my mum's place, anyway!

However, even though my children adore my mum, they wanted to be in London near their schools and friends. The travelling from my mum's place was soon getting too much for them. We had to leave so early in the mornings to get to school and to avoid the traffic jams going into London. In addition, the kids had major exams, which added to the stress, and we had frequent arguments. I felt I had moved from one bad situation to another. It became a nightmare, but I felt I could not be too hard on the kids because of all the stuff they had going on in their lives.

Once we had settled in at my mum's, I signed up with every estate agent in the areas I felt we might move to. Some mornings after dropping the kids off at school, I would park up in the car and fall asleep - I was so tired. I suppose all of the recent traumatic experiences were catching up with me, plus now I was dealing with the divorce.

After doing the things I had to do during the day, on some days I had a few hours to spare. One day, I found a beautiful church in St Johns Wood. I had passed the church many times before, but never stopped to have a look inside. This one particular day I did. The inside of the church was beautiful. Ever since I had given my heart to the Lord I had never found a church I liked, but there was something about this church that I loved. I just had to keep coming back!

I felt really shy at first, walking in there. Not that anyone could see me - I was the only one there for most of the time. But feeling shy, I sat in the pew right at the back and just prayed. I felt this amazing peace. The church became a place I just had to go to after the school runs. After a few times, I moved from the back pew to the middle. I became such a regular that the church caretaker recognised me and would always say, “Morning!”

While sitting in the church, I noticed many people would come in and say their prayers. Some would light a candle; others would just sit and pray. The church had an atmosphere. Probably all churches seem to have a peaceful atmosphere, but to me, there was something special about this church.

I know there are many lost souls and there are many people trying to find God for themselves. When God has a calling on someone's life they might happen to walk into a church and so happen to meet someone who will pray for them. What was nice about this church was that it was always open. These days, not many churches are open all day long for people to go into. Sometimes people just like to be on their own at first and have a silent prayer. They might not want to sit in for a service; they might just want that time alone with God. That was true for me.

After many weeks of going into the church, I felt I began to fit in. Even though I was praying and sitting on my own, the caretaker's morning greeting went from just "Morning!" to "Morning, sweetheart!" to "Morning, babe!" I was also no longer shy about walking into the church. After going from the back pew to the middle row, I now went to the front.

Before I found that church, there was so much going on in my life that I was trying to deal with, that I just prayed about my situation. Although I was praying morning, noon and night, I wasn't hearing from God, I was just asking him for things. But the time in the church gave me time to focus on what God was doing in my life, and this is what Jan meant when she said that God was stripping me down to get me to the place where he wants me to be. If that meant shutting every door so all I could do was focus on his purpose and plan for my life, then so be it. So, through having the time in the church, God started showing me bits about myself.

He took me back over situations and times where I had allowed myself to be bullied, downtrodden, humiliated, controlled and abused. I suppose abuse sums it all up. I felt this presence around me so strong it was beautiful. It was the presence of God's Holy Spirit. I was changing; my life was changing. God's presence through his Holy Spirit was getting stronger in me. Even though some days, some weeks and some months were really hard, I came back stronger so that I could then deal with the next layer.

At times when it got really hard, I just kept trusting in God. His plans bring peace. Isaiah 40:31 says: "Those who trust in the Lord will find new strength. They will soar high on wings like eagles. They will run and not grow weary. They will walk and not faint."

In my whole life I was always busy for everyone else, running here, there and everywhere - but never for myself. I totally gave me to everyone. Even though I was leaving Essex so early for school runs, that time in the church gave me the chance to breathe and sigh for a bit.

Even though my emotions were all over the place, things were changing. I liked the new feelings I was experiencing. Some days I would still have a real good cry, some days I was exhausted, but nothing could stop me from enjoying my new-found spiritual freedom.

I do know that walking with God is not easy. You do have your ups and downs, but you also have God's help. Hebrews 2:18 says: "Since he himself has gone through suffering and testing, he is able to help us when we are being tested."

The difference between my old life and my new one was remarkable. I was getting a confidence I never had, a strengh I never had, a boldness I never had. I started running and getting really fit. I was happy - a happiness inside that I had never felt before.

So the marriage was over, the home was sold, we were settled at my mum's, and the only difficult thing was the travelling - but we were dealing with it. I prayed my prayers, I'd found a church I liked, the divorce was going through, and all I had to do was find a home. It all seemed to be working out perfectly. I thought: "This is it - all the bad is over. Now I've gone through the heartache maybe I will start to see the light. I can deal with my kids screaming at me, they are just releasing their emotions."

But it started to get worse.

My daughter would come running into my room in the middle of the night, demanding: "Get me back to London, my friends are having a party." Or my kids would get me to pick them up, but they would leave me sitting in the car for an hour or two, waiting for them. It was getting out of control. So now I was coming under the control of my own kids! I would never let them down, and they knew it. But because I knew their hearts were broken because of our family break-up, I allowed it all to happen.

So now I had moved from one situation of emotional abuse to another. I could see where all this was going. In life, things you allow to happen become a habit, and so it becomes a normal way of living. But this time it was going to be different. When you let God into your life, he has a plan to change you for the better. He wasn't going to let me repeat the old patterns and be dominated by others. I thought my struggles were over, now that I had escaped my husband and we had a new start in life. But, no, God was not going to let me slip back into my old ways. He began using people and situations to teach me that these are not God's ways - he did not want me to be treated like that. So, even though I was feeling more confident, stronger and bolder, in God's eyes I was still timid and weak. But when we are weak, God can make us strong.

The Apostle Paul learned that our weaknesses are opportunities for God's strength to work in us. In 1 Corinthians 2:3-5 he says: "I came to you in weakness—timid and trembling. And my message and my preaching were very plain. Rather than using clever and persuasive speeches, I relied only on the power of the Holy Spirit. I did this so you would trust not in human wisdom but in the power of God."

So, bit by bit, God was showing me all the wrong behaviour that had brought my life down before, and helping me to change it. He wasn't going to stop now.

After a few weeks at my mum's, things began to get difficult. Even though I was enjoying what I looked like and being out of my old surroundings, I found it really hard to find a flat that I liked. The strain was starting to tell. My mum and I kept arguing, and it all began to get on top of me. No matter what home I looked at, I did not get any sense of wanting to live there. I was constantly looking but nothing grabbed me, and the rows were getting worse. I started to feel so unhappy that I would have settled for a bed-sit!

When I went into the church one day, I walked past all the seats, straight out to the front, right up to the altar where there is a beautiful cross. I said, "Lord, today is the day you have to find me a home. What's happening to me, Lord?" I felt as though I had moved from one bad situation into another. Even if I felt settled for a week, problems would start again with something else. There seemed to be no end to it.

But on that very day that I prayed, I found a new home the same afternoon. I had already seen the flat on the Internet, but it had never caught my eye at all. However, the estate agent said I should take a look, and that morning I would have gone for a bedsit so I had nothing to lose! I arranged to meet the agent within ten minutes, and as soon as I walked into the flat I loved it. It had a beautiful feel. I arranged to go back the next day. I made an offer the same day, and the owners accepted it! I gave praise, thanks and love to the Lord.

Now the ball was rolling, solicitors were involved and we had a moving date. Added to which, the flat was empty, so I was excited about making plans to get all the work done before the kids and I moved in.

However, nothing turned out how I had planned it, the rows at my mum's got worse, and I could do nothing right in my kids' eyes. I could not go on like this! I feel God was teaching me that I needed to take control of my children at that time, but the problem was that I wanted so much for my kids to do well at school that I was prepared to do almost anything. I was also so protective of them that I would never let them travel on trains or buses. I always wanted to be there for them and never to let them down. So as much as God was wanting me to break from being controlled by others, I had other motives that prevented me from dealing with this issue. The problem is that "those who are still under the control of their sinful nature can never please God" (Romans 8:8), and I still had fears that were controlling me - fear of failing my kids, fear of them coming to harm, etc. Fear paralyses us and prevents us from trusting God.

When things get like this I have to remember that I am walking in faith and I have to stop fear from stepping into my life. I recall Psalm 34:4: "I prayed to the Lord, and he answered me. He freed me from all my fears."

I got the keys to the flat on 11th November 2010, and was going to make a start on doing it up. I knew exactly how I wanted it, but as I said, that did not go to according to plan, and I had a terrible row with my mum at the end of November. I had to get the strengh to leave my mum's, but I could not take the kids from a comfortable home to a place that needed a lot of work, not after everything they'd already been through. In addition, my mum totally spoiled my kids and that's what they needed at that time, so I decided to move into the flat on my own, to get it ready for the kids.

I was totally on my own now. It was freezing in the flat, as the central heating had broken down, and I had to sleep on a blow-up bed. I felt so alone and hurt. But I had to make the most of a bad situation, and I knew that God was at work in my life, leading me into the place that he wanted me to be, so I hung on. Besides, where could I turn to, other than to God?

There was nothing at the flat, just myself and this blow-up bed, so I had time to think, time to go over things about myself and how weak I was in so many situations. That said, was it always me being weak or did I just trust everyone too much? Did I think everyone around me was nice, with a good heart? Perhaps I was naïve as well as weak.

When we have problems in life, we can all put on amazing fronts to cover up how the issues hurt us, but if the hurts are still there and are not dealt with, they will keep returning. I believe you have to deal with your issues, whatever they are, in order to free you up to move on to the next one. You can't just keep on putting on a brave face. This is where the stripping down comes in again - it's like starting all over again. And maybe because of our issues we attract certain people and accept certain kinds of behaviour. They might be bullying, controlling, aggressive, nasty, insecure or envious people, but we can't control their ways. It's the way we respond to them that counts - will we let their ways affect our well-being or will we learn how to overcome their influence?

Something might happen in our life that may not have an instant effect - it might keep coming back over time and then have a big impact. Some people learn straight away, but not me. I must have been a slow learner. I had let everything happen in my life. So as hard and as difficult as it was to get to the situation where I was in that flat, I knew I was put there to be taught.

Previously I had thought that if I could just manage to get to my mum's, everything was going to start to be okay. I would start to see the light. But did it work out like that? No. My plans were not God's plans for my life.

Every time I got over one hurdle another one would come. Why? Because I continued to keep letting it all affect me. I needed to learn to control my thoughts and my emotions. Through fear, I was holding on to the 'what ifs' - what if that happened, what if this or that went wrong, what would I do? And so on. So for me, I knew I had to start to take hold of who I wanted myself to be. That was the hardest thing. I did not know who I really was or who I wanted to be. But God was beginning to show me who I should be. And because I knew God was working in my life, I knew that one way or another I was going to get it right.

So me being at that flat with nothing other than a blow-up bed and myself was the only way God could get through to me. At first I did not see it like that, but as time went on I could see it all perfectly clearly. As 2 Timothy 1:9 says, God had a plan for us before we even existed: "For God saved us and called us to live a holy life. He did this, not because we deserved it, but because that was his plan from before the beginning of time—to show us his grace through Christ Jesus."

I'd been through so much heartache but had never really stopped to look at myself. I know now that I never really knew myself or loved myself in any shape or form, and the reason I gave everyone else my time was that I was running away from myself. Now, on my own in that flat, it seemed that all the people in my life had gone, all those I thought I loved, and the friends I cared for. On top of that, all the things that I thought I liked or that I thought made me happy were gone. So here I was. I thought, "What did I do in life to deserve all this?" I took myself back over situations and incidents of my life.

God kept showing me that I had been punishing myself through other people and their behaviour.

As I was going over things of the past, I began to see the truth of this. The smokescreens were being blown away, and I started to see things more clearly. The more God taught me, the more emotions I went through. Every time I passed a mirror I would look in it and call myself a mug or a fool for how I had behaved.

Now that I started to see where I had gone wrong, the tests of whether and how I would change began to arrive.

Chapter Four

MY FIRST TEST

I believe the first test of whether I was really prepared to change was this: speaking up for myself. God brought along the opportunity, and I needed to grasp it.

At the time, I thought I had already got the strength to stand up for myself. But when the test came along, it was obvious that I hadn't. I realised that this was a big problem in my life and I had to overcome it.

So here was the test. Some builders who were recommended to me began work on my home, but as time went on it became clear that they were ripping me off. As the weeks went by it became a nightmare, as they got more and more out of hand, and, rather than speaking up, I made myself ill with the thought of how I was going to deal with the situation. The more they came to my home the more I could not cope with what they were doing, and how they were taking over.

One of my friends was so angry she got her friend, another builder, to come to my home to take a look at what was going on. When he saw their work he wanted their number so he could call them, but I knew it was something that I had to deal with myself. I prayed for God to give me the strength to handle it, and early the next morning I carried all their machinery and tools down to the main entrance, and when they arrived I told them never to come back again.

It was like I was being taught a lesson in wrong and right that I should know anyway, but I just found it really hard to speak up. I was always worried about upsetting everyone, never mind myself, so taking control over my own life and standing up for myself was a big issue I had to deal with. It had been a constant problem in my life.

So, when the next lot of builders came to finish the job, I had to be strong from the start. People who saw my kindness and good nature as a weakness had taken advantage of me in the past, and it had to stop. Thank the Lord, with the new builders I was firm about what I wanted, and the work was done as I asked.

It was emotionally draining to stand up for myself, but I had a peace about it that I never had before. In the past I would have worried over such things, and rather than stand up for myself I would have gone to a park bench and stayed there!

But that was just the first victory in the battle. There was still a war to win. Nothing seemed important anymore. All the things I had worked so hard at had, I felt, all been destroyed at the hands of others, and even myself. And it was my own fault for letting them. I had seriously had enough. I lay down on the blow-up bed and thought back over my life before I knew God.

I had been a top hairdresser. I'd trained for many years in a top London salon - a beautiful salon in one of the nicest streets in London. I worked so hard. I used to start at 8.30 in the morning and most days finish at 11 pm in the evening. With the most amazing training, I took my career to the top. I started doing session work and travelling. I had clients of my own, where I would go to their homes or they would come to me.

When I had children I gave up my session work because I did not want to be away from my kids, so I stuck with my clients. I got to know some of them really well. I would stand up for hours, doing beautiful colours, highlights and cuts. Then it started. "Can I pay in a week?" Once I allowed that, it became easy for them to do it again, or they would put in my hand what they wanted to pay instead of what the true rate was. It was embarrassing to ask for my own money, even though I worked so many hours to get it, so I allowed them to get away with it. And some didn't end up paying at all.

If I did not want to charge someone, it should have been my choice, not theirs, so I felt I was working for nothing. All those years of hard slog, all the hours of hard training, just to give it all away! Whatever their issues were became my problem, but I was to blame because I allowed it. My kindness was taken and abused. I could not speak up.

Besides work, another area where my reluctance to confront people gradually destroyed me was, of course, my marriage.

I always had nice homes, my kids went to lovely schools and always had nice things, but my husband was a terrible flirt and charmer. He constantly tormented me by chatting up other women in front of me. Once again I allowed it. Soon he was regularly flirting with a few friends, and they with him. It got so bad that it became very hurtful, and I became laughable - a joke. I don't even think they were attracted to him; I think it might have just been his lifestyle that attracted them.

The Bible says in 1 John 2:16 that "the world offers only a craving for physical pleasure, a craving for everything we see, and pride in our achievements and possessions."

That verse applied to my husband. When he had the affair that finally split the marriage up (along with other causes), I made a point of going to a see a few of the women he'd flirted with, who I had believed were my friends. God gave me the strength to tell them about their behaviour. I now know that my husband initiated the flirting, even though he said that they started it, but that still doesn't excuse their behaviour as my so-called friends.

Romans 13:13-14 says: "Because we belong to the day, we must live decent lives for all to see. Don't participate in the darkness of wild parties and drunkenness, or in sexual promiscuity and immoral living, or in quarrelling and jealousy. Instead, clothe yourself with the presence of the Lord Jesus Christ. And don't let yourself think about ways to indulge your evil desires."

I felt so angry, not with anyone else but myself - for how I let these people into my home for so long, how I kept them in my life for so long. But I was changing. This was a layer of my life that God was dealing with - he was helping me say 'no' to being abused.

I also went to see the woman who had an affair with my husband ten years previously. I told no one I was going; it was something I just had to do. Even to this day I have never told him. But it showed me more of what he was really like, and helped me find a kind of closure - so that it no longer mattered to me anymore. I arranged to meet her, even though it was really hard for me to confront her. I had kept silent for ten years because of the circumstances, but I had to do it because this woman had totally humiliated me, and I just wanted to let her know that I might not have said anything at the time but I knew all along.

As it happened, she confessed it all and told me what she had done. She said that she had never had any luck, and cried that she never wanted her husband to know. I also know it was done out of jealousy. But it hurt me for years, and I carried the hurt alone. I am a woman who likes to look nice, but during that time when I knew my husband was being unfaithful, I did not care about my appearance; nothing meant anything to me anymore. I felt so downtrodden and betrayed. I don't even think at the time that I wanted to bounce back, not for myself or even for my kids. But when I sat there at her table, all that hurt left me. I knew I could now make a clean break. I had begun crossing my hurts off the list, one by one.

My husband's last affair was pure evil, involving a huge amount of lies and deceit. I had totally had enough of it. Proverbs 5:3-4 warns men not to be snared by immoral women: “For the lips of an immoral woman are as sweet as honey, and her mouth is smoother than oil. But in the end she is as bitter as poison, as dangerous as a double-edged sword.” Proverbs 5:15-16 calls for faithfulness in marriage: “Drink water from your own well—share your love only with your wife. Why spill the water of your springs in the streets, having sex with just anyone?” And Proverbs 5:20-21 warns that what is done in private can be seen by the Lord: “Why be captivated, my son, by an immoral woman, or fondle the breasts of a promiscuous woman? For the Lord sees clearly what a man does, examining every path he takes.”

But as I looked back on it all, I was encouraged by another passage in Proverbs: “Don’t fret because of evildoers; don’t envy the wicked. For evil people have no future; the light of the wicked will be snuffed out” (24:19-20).

I was still alone in the flat, and the blow-up bed had now got a puncture, so I was sleeping on a concrete floor. But I did not care - that’s where I wanted to be at that time. I was experiencing such a relationship with the Holy Spirit that nothing else mattered. I would chuckle to myself. I once lived in a beautiful home with many luxuries like beautiful bathrooms, and sprung beds! Now I was living on a concrete floor, washing in a basin in the kitchen. But if I had been offered a palace at that time I would not have accepted it. Through prayer and loving God, I had a great sense of peace and God's presence, and I wanted more of that - not the material things the world had to offer.

All the people I had known whilst I lived with my husband were gone from my life, but I didn't care. Loneliness was a small price to pay for the joy of getting to know God more. That said, I felt so betrayed by others. But I had no one else to blame except myself. I and I alone was the one who had accepted and allowed this in my life. The whole time I was running from myself, yet needy of others and their acceptance. But as I thought back over this, I asked myself, "Did these people and all the lovely things I had done for them make me happy?" The answer came back: "No." I would always go along with what other people wanted, doing whatever they asked, rather than doing what I wanted or going where I wanted to go. I may have had prior engagements, but if someone controlling called me, I would cancel my own arrangements to be in their company.

So, the reason I failed to speak up was that I was needy, so I became controlled and bullied by others. But now, with God in my life, I can trust him to supply all my needs "from his glorious riches, which have been given to us in

Christ Jesus." (Philippians 4:19). God began to show me that I was getting stronger and stronger in defeating every one of my issues. Today, I speak up in every situation. I no longer allow myself to be bullied. I am no longer needy of the wrong kind of people in my life. I believe that "I can do everything through Christ who gives me strength" (Philippians 4:13).

Gradually, as I thought back over my life and began to confront the areas where I needed to change, even though it sometimes hurt to deal with the issue, God would help me to do it. I would then do some more prayer and worship and enjoying God's presence, and then be struck by something else that I needed to change. Either that, or God would allow something to happen in my life that would cause me to develop the character he wanted to develop in me. Again, this was sometimes painful, but as 1 Peter 5:8-11 says: "Stay alert! Watch out for your great enemy, the devil. He prowls around like a roaring lion, looking for someone to devour. Stand firm against him, and be strong in your faith. Remember that your Christian brothers and sisters all over the world are going through the same kind of suffering you are. In his kindness God called you to share in his eternal glory by means of Christ Jesus. So after you have suffered a little while, he will restore, support, and strengthen you, and he will place you on a firm foundation. All power to him forever! Amen."

So, I thought that speaking up for myself was the lesson I had to learn, and I had done it. That was it. How wrong could I be? It was just the start of what I needed to learn. But it was the biggest lesson of them all.

Chapter Five

HEARING FROM GOD

There was a room in my flat that I would pray in. I felt the Holy Spirit all around the flat but there was something about this room that seemed so right for prayer.

I felt it so much. Even when I was sleeping, I sometimes felt called to pray and spend time with God. It was like someone was knocking, not on the front door but on the door of my heart. When I heard it, I got up and went to the room and prayed. That happened many times. It reminded me of Revelation 3: 20 where Jesus says: "Look! I stand at the door and knock. If you hear my voice and open the door, I will come in, and we will share a meal together as friends."

At times I did not want to get my flat finished because I felt that if anything changed I might lose this experience, and I desperately did not want that to happen.

However, the time came when the new builders came to finish the job left by the first set of 'cowboy' builders. As I said before, this time I would have to speak up and stay in control of what they were doing. So I explained the work to them, and the work was started.

I was happy with the way things were going. This time the builders were very polite and worked well. Things started to take shape, whereas before I had lost heart that the job would ever be done right!

When the builders left on one particular day, I walked into the shower room to see what work had been done. There was a pale blue sheet of plaster board that had been put up. One of the builders had written my name on it, with a love heart next to my name. It spoke volumes to me - not the fact that someone had written it, but the way my name was staring me in the face.

I walked out of the room, but after a while I went back again to look at my name. If I went back once I went back 50 times, and each time I went back I stayed longer. It was another trial for me, another test. I had never, ever loved myself , yet the more I went back in the room the more I started liking the name. It was amazing!

I started thinking, if I could start all over again, what would I have done different in my life? What would I have liked to have been, what direction would I have taken? In my whole life I had never faced myself and thought about who I was and what I should do. I spent all my time giving my talents, creativity, kindness, love and time to everyone else, and ran from me. I had to find myself now. I had allowed life to go by without stopping to look at who or what I was.

So, by seeing my name staring me in the face, I was now taking note of the path I had taken before, and the path I now wanted to walk. Hebrews 12:13 says: "Mark out a straight path for your feet so that those who are weak and lame will not fall but become strong." Proverbs 3:6 adds: "Seek his will in all you do, and he will show you which path to take."

And that's what I did. I laid out all of who I was before God and offered my life's path to him. I wanted to be living to God's agenda, not my own. Left to myself, I had meandered through life, buffeted around by others, with no direction. Putting God in charge would make my path "straight".

The flat was now taking shape and was looking nice. It had a beautiful peace. I had never felt like that about a home before. I prayed so much there, and felt the Holy Spirit when I prayed. He would knock on the door of my heart.

Apart from teaching me things, showing me things about

myself and giving me continuous trials until I made the right response, I began to receive something else from God. One day, someone came to my home and, while they were standing there talking to me, something flashed across my mind. It wasn't a flash of light, it was a picture. I ignored it the first time, but after a few miniutes it happened again, revealing a bit more of the picture.

Recognising that it had begun when this person arrived, I asked if it meant anything to her. She could not believe I knew about the thing I was describing. Neither could I, considering I never really knew this person before. So we started talking about God and she said she was trying to find him, but found it hard. All I could do was tell my own story and explain what God had done for me.

She asked me how to give her heart to the Lord, like I had done. So I told her she needed to pray a prayer to invite him in, and asked if she wanted to say the prayer. It was so emotional for this person, but she said the prayer.

For my own part, I gave little thought as to how God was working this all out because I was just really excited for the person. I hoped and prayed that God would start working in this person the way that he had with me. Then it happened again. Part of someone's life flashed before me once again. I felt prompted to ask the person concerned if it was relevant to them. And again, I was able to lead them in a prayer of commitment to Christ. So now God was not only teaching me about myself, he was using me to reach others!

Every time someone gave their life to the Lord I was so excited for them. I now began to understand how powerful the Holy Spirit is. I found that God's timing is perfect and he will use situations to lead people to salvation. I understood why I was getting the pictures or visions that would come before my eyes - it was because the Holy Spirit was showing me something about the person. It might have been something that happened to them before their salvation, or the fact that they went to a church, or they might have found a cross, or had an unusual dream. It was different for every person, because every person is different, but it was something that God could use to show that he was speaking to them. It went on like this for many months.

Once, when I walked in a shop, the man who owned the shop began talking to me, but something told me that he would be saying the prayer soon. I chuckled to myself and then ignored it for a bit. But the next time I went to the shop, to see if the things I ordered had come in, I got a picture before my eyes. After a while I mentioned it to him. I just told him what I saw. I did not say it was a vision or something from God. But it did bring up something about his life, and we started talking about God. After many months this man got in touch to say the prayer with me, but he couldn't say it. Every time it was arranged, he refused out of fear. He thought that if he gave himself to God, something bad would happen to him - God would wipe him out in some way.

But eventually God showed me what was wrong in this man's life. He also showed me what was going to be good in this man's life. After three long, drawn-out attempts, he finally gave himself to God. It was really hard for him, but praise the Lord - he did it! James 4:7-8 says: "So humble yourselves before God. Resist the devil, and he will flee from you. Come close to God, and God will come close to you."

After a day or two, this man went through prayer for deliverance and was finding it so hard. As I said, everyone has a different walk. But he really was battling with his demons. A few days later I got a call from him saying, "How dare you bring God into my life?! I prefer what I was before." But I knew he was just clearing out his bad stuff that he could not face up to before. He did go back to his old ways for a while, but I believed he would eventually get himself onto God's agenda instead of his own. After he had struggled for many months, I received a text from him on New Year's Day 2012. It said: "It's been hard, but I am glad I did not slide down further. I would never have given my heart to God or trusted him or even spoke to him if I had never met you. You are an angel."

The Bible says: "Anyone who belongs to Christ has become a new person. The old life is gone; a new life has begun! And all of this is a gift from God, who brought us back to himself through Christ" (2 Corinthians 5:17-18).

Well, what can you say, other than praise, thank and love God for setting it all up so that this man could come to Christ? He is now getting his life back on track, and yes, it might have been hard at times, but there will always be trials that we need to go through. Jesus warned: "Here on earth you will have many trials and sorrows. But take heart, because I have overcome the world" (John 16:33).

So this is how my own walk was going with God. Even though I was still going through many trials myself, and still had little battles of hurt that crept back in my life about myself, I discovered that God could use me. I now had an understanding of what God was doing in my life.

One day I was coming back from Essex but missed my turning. I ended up down this beautiful country lane. Right in front of me was a beautiful church, like St Johns Wood

Church. It was open, so I just had to go inside. I walked right to the front and prayed. After being in there for a while, two women walked in the church. I looked round and turned back to finish my prayer. Then something like a voice said to me: "Go and pray for one of them." It happened again. I started saying to myself, "How can you go and approach someone you don't know?" But I did. There was something about the voice that meant I just knew it was God.

So I went up to the two women and said: "I believe I should pray for one of you." They both were happy to be prayed for, but one stood forward and said, "Me!" However, the voice spoke to me again and said, "No, the other one." Well, I had to listen to the Holy Spirit, so I prayed for the one I'd been directed to. Afterwards, she said she could not believe it, because she had just lost her boyfriend through a tragic death, and did not know where to turn, so she came into the church. How amazing was that?! My wrong turn ended up bringing a young woman to God. How wonderful God is! His timing is perfect.

After that, I began to hear from God more frequently. I liked that church, and every time I went to Essex I could not resist going to it to pray, and when I did I could sometimes pray for three or four people in one day at the church. It also started happening at St Johns Wood Church. So in my walk with God I was becoming more sensitive to his Holy Spirit. I was not only hearing God's voice but also being placed in the right places at the right time.

But as I said before, I was still facing many trials myself. I discovered that walking with God is not easy, but it's more than worth it. Jan told me that in the beginning it would be hard, and it was, but I would never give up my walk with God. I love him with all my heart. I still keep in touch with Jan to find out what's happening. She has taught me so much.

Chapter Six

GROWING IN CHRIST

Jan called one day and asked how I would feel about having a full baptism. How could I refuse? It is clearly taught in the Bible that this is something every Christian should do.

Before my baptism I fasted and prayed for a week - eating nothing at all, just drinking water - to ensure that I was spiritually prepared for this big step in my life. I was so excited about the baptism, but did not know what to expect.

On 9 October 2011, I met Jan at the church where the baptism was to take place. The church was packed, and there were about eight people being baptised with me. Before our baptism we each read out our testimonies to the congregation. They were all very moving and every one was different from the others. One by one we went into the water and two people prayed for each of us. I loved every minute of it, standing in this water with two people each side who prayed over my life while I was dipped under the water.

For me, being baptised meant another step closer to God. I felt so uplifted, especially after all the amazing prayers. Galatians 3:27 says: “And all who have been united with Christ in baptism have put on Christ, like putting on new clothes.”

As time went on, I found that my walk with God went through different phases. I might be doing something for a few months or weeks, then something else would happen and I would concentrate on that. Sometimes I was not aware straightaway of what I needed to learn, until the same thing happened a few times, and then I would have an understanding of what I was being shown.

One night I was woken up by God ‘knocking’ on my heart’s door - calling me to pray. As I got up, before I even walked to the room where I pray, I was given three names. Within a matter of weeks, those three people had found salvation in Christ - even in the order I was given! How wonderful it all was, that these people were finding God. When I look back to the things that have happened and how they have happened, I can’t help saying: “Wow! How amazing is God!” Not only have I been taken on so many trials, but lots of people have been saved along the way.

That said, learning is not an easy process. There were

many times during my trials that I had my ‘blanket days’ - times where I just wanted to stay in bed under the blanket and not come out! But even those days were teaching me something. And when I had dealt with what I was being shown, I was able to move on in strength to the next layer of revelation. There were days that were so awful, but I would not give up my faith. So many things had gone from my life and sometimes I felt life was unbearable, but I clung onto my Lord.

Once, when I was in church, I was praying and I heard the church door open. I turned round and there was this very smart man, and words just came out of my mouth. He did not hear me, but I said, “Spirit of darkness.” I thought, “Oh! Where did that come from?!” This man went up to the front to write down a prayer, and then we starting talking. God gave me so many visions about this man. Within two weeks he gave himself to God, praise the Lord! Even though the spirit of darkness may have been at work, God is far more powerful. John 1:5 says: “The light shines in the darkness, and the darkness can never extinguish it.”

I prayed many times for this man, and now he is walking a different path in life, glory to God! We have also become good friends, and later I asked him about the visions I was given for him. Every one was correct. I was on a complete high, thinking this is all amazing, and how wonderful it is that God plans these things and sets it all up. I so enjoyed everything God was showing me and how it was right every time. “For the Lord Most High is awesome. He is the great King of all the earth” (Psalm 47:2). I just loved him with all my heart.

One night I kept seeing this picture of a church I knew, but had never been inside. I always now take notice of the things I am shown, and I believed I was meant to go to this church to pray for someone. I prayed about it, and the picture of the church became as clear as anything.

The next day I had to go to the bank, so I thought I might as well go to the branch near the church. I parked my car and then went into St Johns Wood Church while I was passing it. I thought I might as well go in and quickly say my thanks for the day. A lady who walked in behind me was crying, so we spoke for a bit and I prayed for her.

Afterwards I walked to the other church I believed God had shown me. As I strolled inside, people were coming in and out of the church. But I didn’t feel prompted to pray for any of them. I kept saying, “Lord, where is this person you want me to meet?” I prayed for one lady, but I knew it was not her. Just minutes after she left, an elderly lady walked in. She was immaculately dressed and very well spoken. She was like royalty! When she started speaking to me, I was saying to myself, "Hurry up, someone will be coming in who needs prayer." But this lady asked me if I had ever been to the church before, and I told her I hadn't, so she said, "Let's take a seat." I was getting agitated because I believed she was distracting me from what I was there to do. She then told me that she had never been to that church before either, and she believed she had come to the church to pray for someone!

Well, she started telling me a true story about someone, but it was not until later that I saw that the story explained why she was there. You see, God had given me the picture of the church, and the time to go, but I had believed I was going to pray for someone. In fact, I was the one who ended up being prayed for! That was his purpose and plan. I realised that I shouldn't make assumptions about what God was going to do.

The lady spoke to me about forgiveness. She also said, "Don't you worry, these people who have caused the hurt can lie to others, but they can never lie to God. Forgive them and leave it in the hands of God." When I left the church, I kept saying, "Why? Why?"

When I got home that evening, I sat on my hands and knees in the room I like praying in, forgiving those people.

I thought that I had forgiven everyone before, but had I really? No, not in my heart.

The next morning, when I woke, I felt like I had been in a boxing ring with a champion. I was exhausted. But the prayer was powerful, and letting all the hurt I was carrying go was a release, a relief. So really that was a trial in a day, and it was amazing how God had arranged it.

In fact, he gave me another message that explained that the lady he sent to the church, who prayed for me, was one of God's servants - an angel of forgiveness. When God speaks it is powerful. His words are like no one else's. John 8:47 says: "Anyone who belongs to God listens gladly to the words of God."

A few days later, I was in the car on my way to go shopping when I heard God's voice say, "Go to the church." No, I told myself, it was just me speaking. But then again I heard, "Go to the church." So this time I obeyed and made my way to the church. When I walked in, no one was there, or so I thought. As I began to walk to the front, I heard a voice to the left of me say, "Hello." When I turned, a man was standing there, holding his hat. I said "Hi" and carried on walking to the front, where I prayed. The inner voice of the Spirit prompted me: "Go and pray for him." I resisted because I thought he might be a bit weird, but then the voice came again, saying, “There is no fear under God.” Hebrews 13:6 makes this clear: “So we can say with confidence, ‘The Lord is my helper, so I will have no fear. What can mere people do to me?’”

Besides, it is our loving duty as Christ’s followers to help others wherever we can. Hebrews 13:1-3 says: “Keep on loving each other as brothers and sisters. Don’t forget to show hospitality to strangers, for some who have done this have entertained angels without realising it! Remember those in prison, as if you were there yourself. Remember also those being mistreated, as if you felt their pain in your own bodies.”

Well, when I eventually turned round he was gone, so I ran to the door of the church and went outside, looking for him. There he was, with a small Bible in his hand. I had to trust in God to lead me, so I started by simply asking him if he was OK. The conversation developed and we chatted for a while outside the church, then went back inside. The result? He gave his life to God. Glory to God! He said he had left a prayer in the church a few days previously, asking God to come into his life. He just needed someone to help him ‘over the edge’. He is now walking with God.

When I was praying for him, God gave me the word, "Angel." This time it was "Angel of the heart." He was giving me this kind of message quite a lot now, so I held on to the word and hoped I would get more of an understanding at some point in the future in my walk with God.

The Lord showed me many, many things, sometimes about me and sometimes about others. When I look back I realise how many changes he made in me that I might not have seen at the time. I think, "Wow! God is so good."

One day when I went to the church there was a lady sitting in a pew. As I passed her, she said, "Hello" and we starting talking. She seemed tired and worn out, but God had already shown me that what was wearing her out was not her own problems, it was the weight of what everyone else placed on her shoulders. She was like a shopping bag, carrying what everyone had given her. That said, she told me that she did have a wasting disease. I really felt for this woman and her difficult situation.

God told me to ask about her husband. I did, and she shared the awful story of what had happened to him. I asked if she would like to come to the front of the church with me so I could pray for her there. She said that would be nice, so we walked up to the front. As we did so, I felt this heat all around my hand, like a fire. I held her hand and put my other hand on the centre of her back. I prayed for this woman and asked for her to be released from the pain of the tragic way her husband had been killed, and for her to forgive others for many things. I knew she felt the power of the Holy Spirit, just like I did.

After prayer, she turned and kissed my hand and said, "God, I thank you for this lady and her hands." It was so emotional for her. As she left the church, I watched her as she walked all the way up the aisle. It was like her body had straightened up instead of being weighed down by difficulties. She turned back and said, "God bless you!" I said, "You too!" Our voices echoed down the church. When she left, I asked God what had just happened. The reply came: "You have healing hands."

My walk with God was getting stronger and stronger, even though I was still having my bad days. He was using me in such a way that I could now be just standing next to someone and I would feel this amazing heat from the Holy Spirit. This happened many times.

One day I prayed for a lady and told her that there was an amazing church in her area. She knew where the church was and said she would go along one day and have a look. Many weeks passed and the lady came to mind again. I thought I would go along to the church and see how she was getting on. Once again I was also given the right day to go, so I set off, thinking I was going to see the lady.

When I got there, there was a talk being given. I peered through the glass and a woman was calling me in. She came to the door and said, “Come in, come in, we are just having a talk.” My eyes were only looking for the lady I was thinking of, but she was not there. The woman who called me in sat me at a table with five other women. I sat and studied every one of them. God gave me the word, “Angels”, and he told me what every angel was at the table.

When I was leaving, I explained to the woman who called me inside that I was looking for someone. I described her and she said she might be someone who comes on Sundays. She gave me a big hug and prayed. When I got to my car, I saw that her name tag had stuck to my scarf. I also smelt her perfume on me all day. Once again, I got a message from God to go to the same church. I got in my car and set off without asking God why, but I was thinking it was to see the lady I had prayed for. However, again, that was not God’s plan. The church is an amazing place where they do so much and welcome so many people. It is a great place to enjoy fellowship, but again I didn’t see the lady I had in mind, so I assumed God's direction was just for me to enjoy being there.

In my walk with God I had many trials, many ups and downs, many weeks of tears, anger and mixed emotions, and times when I wanted to just hide away under my blanket. But through them all, God was strengthening me. As soon as I had dealt with one, he showed me another. At the beginning when I moved in with my mum I thought it was all going to be fine there, but no, God wanted me on my own, so he could work on me.

I always remember Jan's words: "Imagine yourself like an onion. As you peel back the layers bit by bit, eventually there is nothing left." That's what was happening to me, layer by layer. If I stayed around certain people and things, I was never going to become who I really wanted to be, or more importantly, who God wanted me to be. And through my trials, as I got stronger, God gave me the gift of being able to pray for others. At first I was not aware of that, but the more it happened the more I understood what God was doing. Then he gave me the gift of hearing him, and then the gift of healing hands. Each gift is given to us to use within his timing, for his plan.

1 Corinthians 12:4-11 explains the spiritual gifts: "There

are different kinds of spiritual gifts, but the same Spirit is the source of them all. There are different kinds of service, but we serve the same Lord. God works in different ways, but it is the same God who does the work in all of us. A spiritual gift is given to each of us so we can help each other. To one person the Spirit gives the ability to give wise advice; to another the same Spirit gives a message of special knowledge. The same Spirit gives great faith to another, and to someone else the one Spirit gives the gift of healing. He gives one person the power to perform miracles, and another the ability to prophesy. He gives someone else the ability to discern whether a message is from the Spirit of God or from another spirit. Still another person is given the ability to speak in unknown languages, while another is given the ability to interpret what is being said. It is the one and only Spirit who distributes all these gifts. He alone decides which gift each person should have."

Every time I received a gift I was obedient to God in using it. I listened to the Holy Spirit. I aspire to follow Paul's instruction to the Corinthian church in 2 Corinthians 9:13-15: "As a result of your ministry, they will give glory to God. For your generosity to them and to all believers will prove that you are obedient to the Good News of Christ. And they will pray for you with deep affection because of the overflowing grace God has given to you. Thank God for this gift too wonderful for words!”

Chapter Seven

GOD'S GIFT OF PEOPLE

Even though many people disappeared from my life after I found faith in Jesus, God brought new people to me. I made so many really nice friends, and even some friends from my past come back - the ones God wanted for me. But there are others I will probably never see again, as God has taken me away from them so that I cannot be influenced by them anymore.

A good friend of mine sent me this beautiful email during the time God was clearing out the rubbish in my life:

> People come into your life for a reason, a season or a lifetime. When you know which one it is, you will know what to do for that person.
>
> When someone is in your life for a reason, it is usually to meet a need you have expressed. They have come to assist you through difficulty, to provide you with guidance and support, to aid you physically, emotionally or spiritually.
>
> They may seem like a God-send - and they are. They are there for the reason you need them to be. Then, without any wrongdoing on your part or

at an inconvenient time, this person will say or do something to bring the relationship to an end. Sometimes they die, sometimes they walk away, sometimes they act up and you have to take a stand.

What we must realise is that our need has been met, our desire fulfilled, so their work is done. The prayer you sent up has been answered, so move on.

Some people come in your life for a season, because your turn has come to share, grow or learn. They bring you an experience of peace or make you laugh. They may teach you something you have never done.

They usually give you an unbelievable amount of joy... believe it, it is very real, but only for a season.

Lifetime relationships teach you lifetime lessons - things you must build upon in order to have a solid emotional foundation. Your job is to accept the lesson, love the person and put what you have learned to use in all other relationships and areas of your life.

It is said that love is blind but friendship is clairvoyant.

Thank you for being part of my life, whether you were a reason, a season or a lifetime.

When it comes to letting people in my life, I now know what I want because through God I have got to know myself more, as a person. Even the friends that came back from my old life were the ones God brought back. They were the ones I know in my heart that I was happy with and had good times with.

Another friend sent me this poem:

> The time will come with elation.
> You will greet yourself arriving at your own front door.
> In your own mirror, each will smile at the other, and say, 'Welcome, sit here and eat.'
> You will love again the stranger who was yourself.
> Give wine, give bread, give back your heart to itself, to the stranger who has loved you all your life, whom you ignored for another.

One Sunday afternoon I was in Essex and went into a church on my way home from visiting my friends - a big church with the most amazing ceiling. I always go right to the front and pray. While praying, the door of the church opened behind me. I looked round, and a lady walked in with a boy. I carried on praying, but I felt them walking close to me. The lady said, "How beautiful that looks, standing there, praying." I turned around to talk, and I felt myself getting emotional - so much so that tears were running down my face. My tears were not for the lady, they were for the young boy.

The lady told me that they had come to look at a house in the area and wanted to come to the church. I asked the lady if the boy was her son. "Yes," she said. I asked if I could pray for him. She replied: "Yes, I have been praying for this day." I took him right to the front of the church. God gave me the words, "Abused" and "Bullied", along with so much more. I asked the Lord to guide me all through this prayer. I felt the Holy Spirit's presence so powerfully - more than ever before.

The boy had been a victim, so much that he could hardly speak, due to fear. When we finished praying, God broke all the negative emotions that he was carrying, one by one. I believe he received instant deliverance. All the praise, thanks and love to the Lord! Glory to God!

My trials seem to be different now than in those early days. I was so emotional, I had so many ups and downs. But God was dealing with my heart, and sometimes I never knew where all the tears had come from! But they were there. There was even anger inside me. I am not an angry person at all, but it was there. And still I had the 'blanket days' where I wanted to shut myself off from the world and everyone. But having faith in God made me deal with every one of the emotions.

Chapter Eight

CAREER OR CALLING?

As time went on I felt I wanted to get a different kind of job. I decided on what kind of work I wanted to do, and got my CV together. I believed it was very interesting and showed my creative talent, so I just kept sending it out.

But I never got a single response.

I sat with my daughter and went over the CV. She said, "Mum, if I were a boss I would really consider you." I said, "You're only saying that because I am your mum." "No, it's true, Mum!" she answered. Well, if she was right, why wasn't I getting any requests to come for an interview?

One day I was walking up the high street and I saw an advert in the window for staff, full-time or part-time. I thought I would love to work in there for a change. Walking to my car, I got excited as I imagined myself working in this beautiful shop. I got to my car and drove round to the church. One of my friends was there who I had become friends with through prayer. I told him about the job and he said, "Go for it, but don't waste your talents."

That night I got all excited, thinking about the change and trying to see myself working at the shop. I was convincing myself that I would soon be working there. When I got up the next day I was feeling so confident. I got all ready and drove down to the shop, parking nearby. But when I got there the sign was no longer in the window! I thought they might have removed it to clean the window, so I walked in and asked about the job they had advertised in the window. "Sorry, it's gone," the lady said. I could not believe it.

I drove straight to church and walked right in. You could hear my heels stomping up to the front of the church. "Lord, what's happening?! I really want a different job, and I wanted that one."

After many minutes of looking down and praying, I heard a voice say, "Enough." I thought, "Enough? I need you to be more specific than that, Lord." I then got the whole picture.

From the moment I gave my heart to God I had never turned back to my previous life. I had been taken from a life of abuse, constant affairs, false friends, humiliations and mental torture and been given a new life. Before I knew God, I may have had many materials things, but I had no self-worth, self-respect, strength, happiness or confidence. So I had lost my life in order to find it. As Jesus says in Mark 8:35: "If you try to hang on to your life, you will lose it. But if you give up your life for my sake and for the sake of the Good News, you will save it."

In all my time with God, I had - in a way - been running from myself. Although I had been through many trials, all my prayers were for other people. I was not listening to God when it came to myself, my path and the visions God had given me for my life. That's why the voice of God's Spirit said, "Enough."

When I came home that day, I went over the visions I had been given over time, and realised how I was helping others with the circumstances of their lives yet ignoring God's direction for my own life. That's why I was getting nowhere with my job applications, because I was not considering the path God had planned for me. You see, when God wants you to walk in a specific direction, he will close all the other doors so that eventually you only have God's path left to follow. God had something else in mind for me. As Psalm 37:23-24 says, he does indeed guide us: "The Lord directs the steps of the godly. He delights in every detail of their lives. Though they stumble, they will never fall, for the Lord holds them by the hand."

Along the spiritual path I was treading, it came to a point

where there was a big change for me. I came to a place where the worst of everything was over. God had taken me through many trials, using situations and people to teach me things about myself. But as I was walking through all these tunnels of darkness I was slowly emerging into the light. Ephesians 5:8 says: “For once you were full of darkness, but now you have light from the Lord. So live as people of light!”

All the hard trials were over and now God was moving fast in my life. That’s why he sent the first Angel of forgiveness, and kept giving me the word “Angels” - five times, in fact. Those words taught me five major things about myself, the final things I needed to move into God’s purpose and plan for my life.

In the same week as the Angel words, the job experience and the word “Enough”, I was woken up in the middle of the night and given the word, “Exodus 13:4”. So I looked up Exodus 13:4 and it says this: “On this day in early spring, in the month of Abib, you have been set free.” And that’s exactly how I felt at the time. I had been set free from all the trials, the hurts and upsets, and I was seeing amazing changes in my life. My faith was stronger than ever before, and when I look back at the way it has all happened I can’t help but say how great is the Almighty God, my Lord and my Saviour.

If you are going through struggles and trials, never give up on God. The Bible says that "we work hard and continue to struggle, for our hope is in the living God, who is the Saviour of all people and particularly of all believers" (1 Timothy 4:10).

Different circumstances bring different people closer to God, but not all continue on the right path. Many people who I have prayed for have turned towards God for a while, and might feel great for a time, but they are not prepared to make the necessary changes in their life. Others want it all to happen in an instant, and when things don't work out straight away they lose faith, or they find it hard to completely trust in God. Others might start out well, but when something doesn't work out in their favour they start blaming God and go back to their old ways. The Bible warns against this: "When people escape from the wickedness of the world by knowing our Lord and Saviour Jesus Christ and then get tangled up and enslaved by sin again, they are worse off than before" (2 Peter 2:20).

Chapter Nine

DON'T GIVE UP!

When you give your life to God it should be something you want to do wholeheartedly. Jesus warned us that "anyone who puts a hand to the plough and then looks back is not fit for the Kingdom of God" (Luke 9:62). And when God places a calling on your life, you should follow it for Jesus' sake and not for your own benefit. Yes, God will bless us if we trust him, but we don't follow God for his blessing, we follow him because of our love for him and his love for us. God knows our motives and our inner thoughts. We might not show our motives to others but we can't hide them from God - he sees our heart. As 1Thessalonians 2:4 says, "Our purpose is to please God, not people. He alone examines the motives of our hearts."

So, when you give yourself to God wholeheartedly, I believe he gives you a key. Not just any key, but a golden key! This key is the ability to listen to God. He will then start showing you things in your life and take you on your walk with him. It's your responsibility to listen and pray for understanding, so that you can take the right path. We all make mistakes and make a wrong turn from time to time, but keep focused on God and doing right by him and he will get you back on the path.

You may have to face trials along the way, but look for an understanding of what the trial has to teach you. Be patient and be encouraged that God is at work in you. In 1 Peter 6:9 we read: “So be truly glad. There is wonderful joy ahead, even though you have to endure many trials for a little while. These trials will show that your faith is genuine. It is being tested as fire tests and purifies gold—though your faith is far more precious than mere gold. So when your faith remains strong through many trials, it will bring you much praise and glory and honour on the day when Jesus Christ is revealed to the whole world.”

So when all these trials arise, you have to keep trusting God to take you through them, and in the end you will have a peace that only God can give.

I have been quite shocked on my walk by how many people are so frightened of God, rather than being at peace. I fear God, and he is the only person we should fear, but it's a healthy kind of fear. The fear I am talking about is unhealthy - it gets in the way of our relationship with God. I would never be afraid to stand before God, but many people are. Some people are afraid of God because they worry that they are not really saved. In that case, they need to take God at his word. He says in 1

Peter 1:23: “For you have been born again, but not to a life that will quickly end. Your new life will last forever because it comes from the eternal, living word of God.”

Often the reason people are afraid of God is guilt. But if we are living under guilt it’s either because we have not repented or because we do not believe that God loves us so much that he forgives us - whatever we have done. Again, we have to trust God’s Word that he has forgiven us.

When some give themselves to God they have this awful fear that he might have seen all the wrong things they have done. Well, they are right, he has seen it all - and he still loves us! And because he loves us, we have no need to be afraid. Scripture says that perfect loves casts out all fear: “Such love has no fear, because perfect love expels all fear. If we are afraid, it is for fear of punishment, and this shows that we have not fully experienced his perfect love” (1 John 4:18). So we shouldn’t be afraid, because God loves us perfectly. In fact, Scripture says that Christ died for us while we were still sinners (Romans 5:8). He didn’t wait for us to repent first. God knows everything about us, whether we follow him or not.

If you still have fear, meditate on these words from Romans: “Since we have been made right in God’s sight by faith, we have peace with God because of what Jesus Christ our Lord has done for us. Because of our faith, Christ has brought us into this place of undeserved privilege where we now stand, and we confidently and joyfully look forward to sharing God's glory" (Romans 5:1-2).

Others find it hard to follow God because, as I said before, they want it all to happen overnight. But God works to his own schedule, not ours. So you have to be patient, trusting and having faith that his will will be done. As hard as it gets for you, and as many doors close further on the walk, you will see the light and new doors will open. In the end, the Christian life all comes down to loving God and having faith. If we worry about things or have doubts, we are not having faith or trusting in God. Proverbs 3:5-6 says: "Trust in the Lord with all your heart; do not depend on your own understanding. Seek his will in all you do, and he will show you which path to take."

If you follow God you can have an unbelievable peace - a supernatural calm, even though everything around you might be falling apart. Philippians 4:6-7 says: "Don't worry about anything; instead, pray about everything. Tell God what you need, and thank him for all he has done. Then you will experience God's peace, which exceeds anything we can understand. His peace will guard your hearts and minds as you live in Christ Jesus."

If you have faith, trust and love for him, I believe you can be healed from anything. Psalm 91:14-16 says: "The Lord says, 'I will rescue those who love me. I will protect those who trust in my name. When they call on me, I will answer; I will be with them in trouble. I will rescue and honour them. I will reward them with a long life and give them my salvation.'" Amen!

How true it is, that from the moment you get on God's agenda and not your own, you feel a wonderful lift. It's amazing to walk life with God - like nothing else. I have seen incredible things, like miracles, and heard amazing stories. I've been through many lows and many highs, but when you welcome God in your life, it is worth every one of the trials and difficulties to see the fulfilment of the purpose that God has for your life. As Galatians 6:9 says: "So let's not get tired of doing what is good. At just the right time we will reap a harvest of blessing if we don't give up."

Through my many trials and sorrows I have never given up my faith, ever. Everything that I lost in order to pursue God he has restored to me - every single thing. My self-worth, my self-respect, my strength, friendships, happiness, laughter... So all my trials were worth it.

Romans 5:3-5 says: "We can rejoice, too, when we run into problems and trials, for we know that they help us develop endurance. And endurance develops strength of character, and character strengthens our confident hope of salvation. And this hope will not lead to disappointment. For we know how dearly God loves us, because he has given us the Holy Spirit to fill our hearts with his love."

For me, I am going to hold onto my key - I am going to keep listening and opening the doors God wants me to open and close the doors he wants closed. And if I get it wrong, I will bring it before him and he will put me back on the right path. I know no one is perfect and we all make mistakes, and there are times for everything...

> For everything there is a season,
>   a time for every activity under heaven.
> A time to be born and a time to die.
>   A time to plant and a time to harvest.
> A time to kill and a time to heal.
>   A time to tear down and a time to build up.
> A time to cry and a time to laugh.
>   A time to grieve and a time to dance.
> A time to scatter stones and a time to gather stones.
>   A time to embrace and a time to turn away.
> A time to search and a time to quit searching.

A time to keep and a time to throw away.
A time to tear and a time to mend.
A time to be quiet and a time to speak.
A time to love and a time to hate.
A time for war and a time for peace.
(Ecclesiastes 3:1-8)

But in all my times I pray that God will be with me through everything.

I will take note of every vision he has given me for my life.

I will always try to be on God's agenda, following his purpose and plan for the path he wants me to take.

I will keep listening and serving God in every way he wants me to.

Whoever he puts in my path for prayer I will pray for, wherever God places me I will be... all glory to God.

I will join the heavenly beings in honouring the Lord: "Honour the Lord, you heavenly beings; honour the Lord for his glory and strength. Honour the Lord for the glory of his name. Worship the Lord in the splendour of his holiness" (Psalm 29:1-2).
And I will keep praying for those I personally know who

have given their hearts to God, for them to be patient in their walk and not to throw away their keys. And I will keep praying for those who not only need God in their lives but those who want God in their life, who are searching in the hope that they find him.

I will keep praising and thanking and loving God because of all the great things he has done.

I will keep trusting him even when I can't see the reason why things are happening, because "we know that God causes everything to work together for the good of those who love God and are called according to his purpose for them" (Romans 8:28).

I thank God every day for all my trials and everyone who played a part in my trials, whether they were good to me or not, because God brings good out of bad. Out of sadness he has brought gladness, out of jealousy and envy he has brought self-worth, and out of darkness he has made light.

I don't base my worth on people's opinions of me and how they have acted towards me anymore. My value comes from who I am in Christ.

So I am going to keep praising, thanking and loving God

for this wonderful journey. I am going to keep praising and loving him for all the wonderful blessings that he has given me, and I am going to keep going forward with God. Whatever test I have to go through, I will be patient. James 1:12 says: "God blesses those who patiently endure testing and temptation. Afterward they will receive the crown of life that God has promised to those who love him."

I will never give up what I have been taught and never forget what I have experienced on my walk.

I will stay in God's kingdom and not be of the world.

I will endeavour to do everything in an attitude of love, because only "three things will last forever—faith, hope, and love—and the greatest of these is love" (1 Corinthians 13:13).

I can truly say with the Psalmist, "The Lord Most High is awesome. He is the Great King of all the earth" (Psalm 47:2).

> "And I am convinced that nothing can ever separate us from God's love. Neither death nor life, neither angels nor demons, neither our fears for today nor our worries about tomorrow—not

> even the powers of hell can separate us from God's love." (Romans 8:38)

God bless you!

www.ingramcontent.com/pod-product-compliance
Ingram Content Group UK Ltd.
Pitfield, Milton Keynes, MK11 3LW, UK
UKHW020415250726
13967UKWH00007B/2658

9 780956 686473